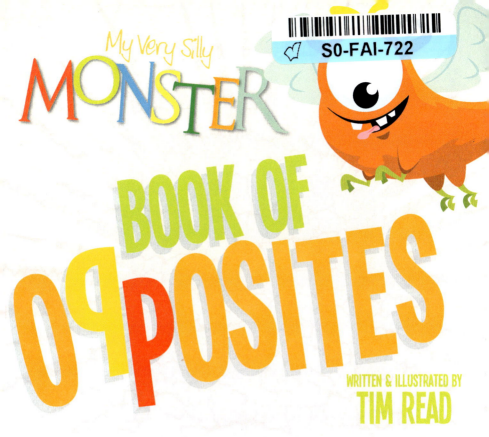

My Very Silly MONSTER BOOK OF OPPOSITES

WRITTEN & ILLUSTRATED BY
TIM READ

For all the Super heroes in the world teaching kids right from wrong, how to look up and not down, and the value in being kind instead of mean... Thank you so very much for being a positive force in kid's lives.

Teachers, Librarians, Police Officers, First Responders, Fire Fighters, Parents, Clergy...the list goes on and on. - T.R.

My Very Silly Monster Book of Opposites
Text copyright © 2017 Tim Read
Illustration copyright © 2017 Tim Read

ISBN-13: 978-1975705800
ISBN-10: 1975705807
Visit us at: www.MyVerySillyMonster.com

Sammi has Small horns.

Billie's horns are Big.

Buddie's back is Bumpy.

Smedley's belly is Smooth.

Hanna is Happy.

Sal is Sad.

Holly likes her cocoa Hot.

Cole likes his snacks Cold.

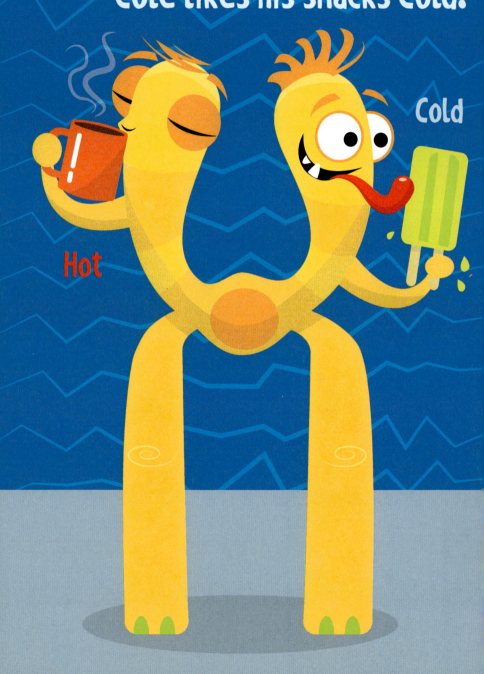

Tommy is tall.

Shilo is short.

Ian is In Molly's mouth.

Ha Ha! Silly Molly.
Ian is now Out of Molly's mouth.

Darla is hiding in the Dark.

Found you! Now Darla is in the Light.

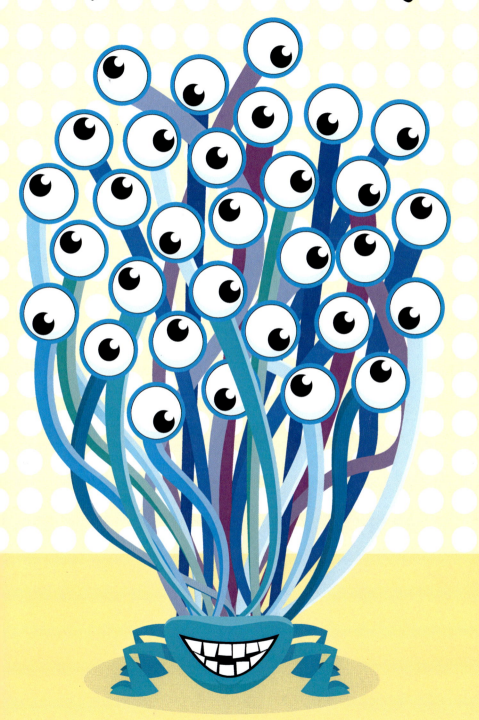

Shirly's tail is Short.

Logan's tail is Long.

Mo has More eyes.

Lexie has Less eyes.

Niko is Near.

Frank is Far.

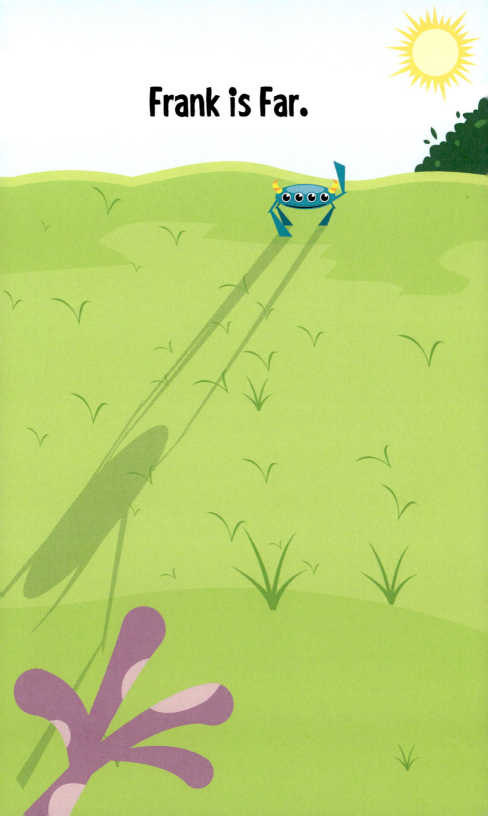

Olly is sitting On Otto.

Ouch! Olly fell Off Otto.

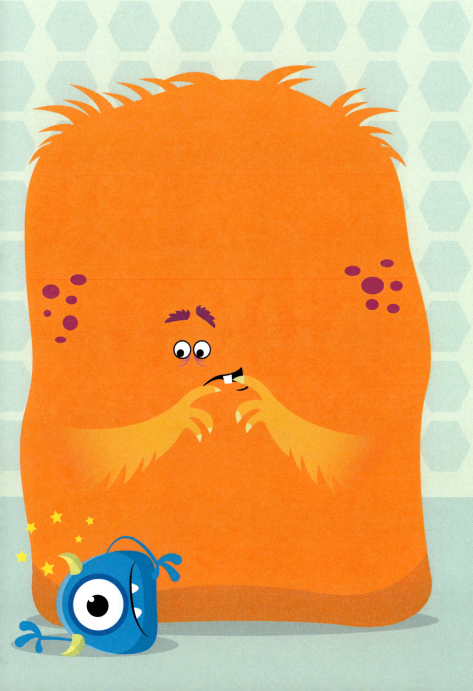

Stanley is Strong.

Wes is Wet.

Dru is Dry.

Oby is Over Unga.

Unga is Under Oby.

Hilda is flying High.

Lou is crawling Low.

Alan's eyes are Apart.

Toni's eyes are Together.

Eight of Owen's eyes are Open.

Eight of Owen's eyes are Closed.

Ellen is Excited.

Bo is Bored.

Before
All
Bad
Bottom
Laugh
Open
Afraid
Dim
Stiff
Sweet
Sunny
Heavy
Round
Messy

Now that you know what opposites are, can you draw a Very Silly Monster opposite of your own? Pick a word from the list and draw the opposite.